This book is dedicated to the Nederlandse Dwergautoclub (DWAC) in celebration of 15 years of enthusiastic commitment to the Microcar cause.
Why such strange and quirky cars encourage good humour is easy to understand, but the running of a car club where good humour, courtesy, gentleness and willingness to help predominate is no small achievement.
Our congratulations to a small-car club with a big heart!

Other books of interest to enthusiasts available from Veloce -

• Colour Family Album titles •
Citroën 2CV: The Colour Family Album by Andrea & David Sparrow
Citroën DS: The Colour Family Album by Andrea & David Sparrow
Bubblecars & Microcars: The Colour Family Album by Andrea & David Sparrow
Bubblecars & Microcars (More!): The Colour Family Album by Andrea & David Sparrow
Lambretta: The Colour Family Album by Andrea & David Sparrow
VW Beetle: The Colour Family Album by Andrea & David Sparrow
Vespa: The Colour Family Album by Andrea & David Sparrow

• Other titles •
Alfa Romeo. How to Power Tune Alfa Romeo Twin Cam Engines by Jim Kartalamakis
Alfa Romeo Giulia GT & GTA Coupe by John Tipler
Alfa Romeo Modello 8C 2300 by Angela Cherrett
Alfa Romeo Owner's Bible by Pat Braden
Bugatti 46 & 50 - The Big Bugattis by Barrie Price
Bugatti 57 - The Last French Bugatti by Barrie Price
Chrysler 300 - America's Most Powerful Car by Robert Ackerson
Cobra - The Real Thing! by Trevor Legate
Daimler SP250 (Dart) V-8 by Brian Long
Fiat & Abarth 124 Spider & Coupé by John Tipler
Fiat & Abarth 500 & 600 by Malcolm Bobbitt
Lola T70 by John Starkey
Mazda MX5/Miata Enthusiast's Workshop Manual by Rod Grainger & Pete Shoemark
MGA by John Price Williams
MGB (4cyl), How To Power Tune by Peter Burgess
MGB. How To Give Your MGB V-8 Power by Roger Williams
MG Midget & A-H Sprite, How To Power Tune by Daniel Stapleton
MGs, Making by John Price Williams
Mini Cooper - The Real Thing! by John Tipler
Morgan, Completely - Three Wheelers 1910-52 by Ken Hill
Morgan, Completely - Four Wheelers 1936-68 by Ken Hill
Morgan, Completely - Four Wheelers from 1968 by Ken Hill
Morris Minor, The Secret Life of by Karen Pender
Motorcycling in the '50s by Jeff Clew
Nuvolari: When Nuvolari Raced ... by Valerio Moretti
Porsche 356 by Brian Long
Porsche 911R, RS & RSR by John Starkey
Rolls-Royce Silver Shadow & Bentley T-Series by Malcolm Bobbitt
Singer, The Story by Kevin Atkinson
Triumph Motorcycles & The Meriden Factory by Hughie Hancox
Triumph TR6 by William Kimberley
V8 Short Block, How To Build For High Performance by Des Hammill
VW Beetle - the Rise from the Ashes of War by Simon Parkinson
VW Karmann Ghia by Malcolm Bobbitt
Weber & Dellorto Carburetors, How To Build & Power Tune by Des Hammill

First published in 1997 by Veloce Publishing Plc., 33 Trinity Street, Dorchester, Dorset DT1 1TT, England. Fax 01305 268864.

ISBN 1 874105 72 3
© Andrea Sparrow, David Sparrow and Veloce Publishing Plc 1997

Readers with ideas for automotive books, or books on other transport or related hobby subjects, are invited to write to the editorial director of Veloce Publishing at the above address.

British Library Cataloguing in Publication Data -
A catalogue record for this book is available from the British Library.

Typesetting (Avant Garde), design and page make-up all by Veloce on Apple Mac.

Printed in Hong Kong.

ANDREA & DAVID SPARROW

VELOCE PUBLISHING PLC
PUBLISHERS OF FINE AUTOMOTIVE BOOKS

THANKS

All of the photographs in this book were made with Leica R6 cameras, with lenses ranging from 16mm fisheye to 400mm. The film used throughout was Fuji Velvia.

People are often curious about cameras and, when they are set up on tripods, there are frequent requests to "have a quick look." People are often surprised by what they see when they peer into the viewfinder - "It looks different, just like a picture" is a common reaction. Then the conversation turns to what made me choose Leicas, and the answer is always the same. The fact is that, once I started looking through a Leica my photographic view of life was changed forever. Perhaps it was partly the selective light metering on my first Leicaflex; the slow and deliberate procedure that made careful thought a prerequisite to taking a photograph. It was a revelation. Best of all, whatever you asked of this system - shooting into the light or lit from the side, indoors or out - it delivered with no fuss or bother. I have convinced cynical clients who previously would accept film formats no smaller than 6x6 that, with a Leica, 35mm is fine.

However, it took more than just cameras and film to make the pictures in this book: thanks are due to the owners of the cars featured, particularly members of the DWAC and especially Sjoerd ter Burg. On a rainy, dark day, star member Henk Kleinendorst and I went in search of the Belcar featured in this book (and the Shelter and Janus which appeared in the original book). Soaked to the skin, but uncomplaining, we found locations and put cars in front of them, daunted only by the Belcar which we had to push everywhere because it was not running.

The UK photo sessions were also noteworthy. Malcolm Clement's Scootacar Mk2 was photographed in his drive, while Nigel Bickle's Mk1 was driven to a location some miles from its home. Malcolm Thomas was outstanding, bringing his Peel P50 and Trident to Windsor on a trailer and then pushing them into various positions on a very cold winter Sunday. Bob Perton suffered the indignity of having his Nobel photographed at a fairground - and looking very much at home there -

but stayed cheerful. I must also thank Barry Rossiter and Brian Perry for their help and patience in making available their red Messerschmitts for the cover shoot: once again the day was cold and wet, but they persevered with good grace. The session with

Lawrence House's Velam was also extraordinary because the two models - like Jade Bond with the Frisky - are clearly mad, partly because of the cold they endured and partly because of the crazy micro-mania stories with which Lawrence entertained us over coffee. I must also thank Mike Webster (whose BSA Ladybird appeared in the original book) for being constantly helpful, as was Jean Hammond.

I must thank a man whose coffee pot I have drunk dry, and for whom nothing was too much trouble. I photographed his Messerschmitt KR for the original book and his Tg500 for this one when he arranged a session at Brooklands. Colin Archer is an enthusiast of the first degree, his devotion to Microcars is second to none. When I first met Colin he was restoring a BMW 600 which we photographed nearly eighteen months later, thanks to permission from its then soon-to-be new owner, Alan Town.

My thanks to Colin Archer, Alan Town, Brian Perry, Barry Rossiter, Lawrence House, Malcolm Thomas, Bob Purton, Sarah Meech, Patrick Pellen, Henk Kleinendorst, Winfrid Jones, Mike Webster, Linda Baldwin, Jo Smith, Sylvia Buckerfield, Sara Bloyce, Jean Hammond, Sjoerd ter Burg, Allan Ellis, Jade Bond, Nigel Bickle, Malcolm Clement, Hans Allers, Peter Highton, Ron Crawley, Vic Smits, the Auto Trom Museum (Rosmalen) and the Brooklands Museum.

CONTENTS

INTRODUCTION

In the introduction to the first volume of *Bubblecars & Microcars* I was anxious to point out that the book did not set out to be an encyclopedia of makes and models. Exactly the same goes for this one. The cars featured within these pages are a selection from many - another handful of members of the microcar band, with common links and diverse stories.

Of those cars featured here, the Messerschmitt Tiger, Peel 50 and BMW 600 have siblings that appeared in the first book, and the Velam a first cousin. The Messerschmitt owes some of its style to the aircraft industry, the Fuldamobil owed its fledgling looks to a caravan manufacturer. The BMW 600 was fitted

with cunning universal joints to move the steering works out of the way when you wanted to get out - the Frisky had instrumentation that resolutely stayed put and skinned your legs for you when you tried the same manoeuvre. The Goggomobil can be ranked among the successes - while the Spatz narrowly avoided being a total disaster. Interestingly the Scooter car falls halfway between these two; it had everything going for it,

but its potential was never maximised.

In the history of microcars, the going often gets tough even before production gets going. Fibreglass stresses, glass cracks, wood proves just not strong enough. But everyone had to start somewhere, even Herr Daimler and Herr Benz. Whenever something really creative and inventive appears on the scene, it's a fair bet that there was a period of risk-taking for someone somewhere along the line. And, implicit in any risk, is the possibility of success or failure. The microcar builders all had something; in some cases it was first class engineering skills - and in others, it was first class enthusiasm!

MESSERSCHMITT TIGER

1

When sales figures for the three-wheeled Messerschmitt began to fade, the company was faced with a major problem. The German government had put serious money into the company with the intention of using its expertise to help re-establish the country's aircraft industry. But the intention had most definitely not been to keep afloat a non-profitable subsidiary making little cars for a dwindling market. Eventually the car-making part of

Messerschmitt's business was taken over by the state of Bavaria, which split it into saleable units and then went in search of deals.

The factory facility at Regensburg was bought by Fritz Fend, inventor of the original Messerschmitt, and Valentine Knott, a prominent businessman. They wanted to build a small sportscar which, although built in the Messerschmitt mould, would attract a new type of customer. Although the three-

The eyes have it ...

Maybe not quite the sportscar it was intended to be, nevertheless the Tiger was fun to drive and did have a sporty feel.

wheeler had not been selling at all well in the years immediately prior to the Fend/Knott takeover, they had provided a firm reputation on which to build this new venture. Public imagination had been caught by record-breaking runs at the Hockenheim circuit, and enough of the *Kabinrollers* had been built and sold to satisfied owners for good words to be spread. But as far as creating a totally new model was concerned, low cost was going to be high up the list of priorities. There was absolutely no way that it was going to be possible to start from scratch with a new model. Instead, the existing three-wheeler was modified by the addition of a second rear wheel and the track was widened slightly.

The new car was presented to the public at the Frankfurt Motor Show in 1957; it went into production in its dome-topped form the following year and a convertible version appeared in 1959. Called the Tg500 by its manufacturer, the new car became generally known as the Tiger. Although it did share its basic shape with its older three-wheeled brother, the Tiger was a different sort of animal. It was fitted with a Sachs 493cc two-cylinder two-stroke engine which delivered 20bhp and gave the car a top speed of over 85mph!

Sidelight detail. A miniature work of art.

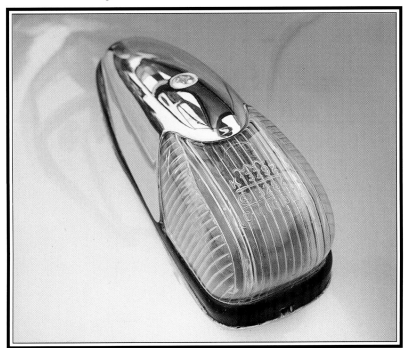

Opposite - Tiger stripes. Although only 300 or so were ever made, Tiger owners are dedicated to their unique cars.

The Sachs 493cc two-cylinder two-stroke engine which gave the Tiger a top speed in excess of 85mph.

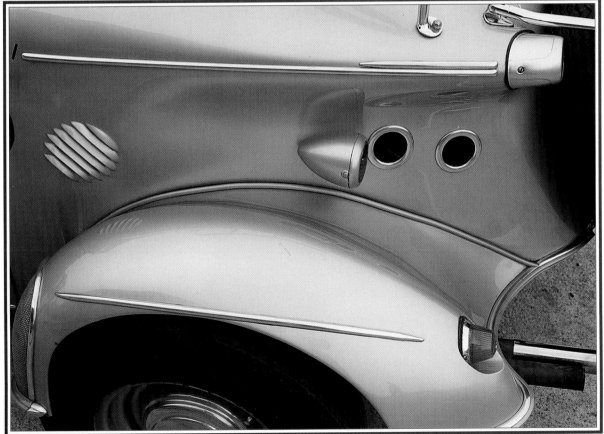

Detail of the Tg500's rear wing area. All the Tg500s which are known to exist have been traced and painstakingly checked and listed in the Tg500 Official Register.

Opposite - The Tg500 was not just the well-loved Kabinroller wearing a new set of clothes - Fend intended it to reach a completely new market.

A beautiful silver Tiger with "500" license plate; after Germany, more Tg500s were sold in the UK than anywhere else in the world. Whichever way you look at it, that canopy cannot belong to anything other than a Messerschmitt.

One of the major criticisms levelled at the Tiger concerned the amount of interior accommodation - the new car was an adaptation of the existing three-wheeler so space was very limited. In an effort to keep costs down, interior fittings were the same as in the three-wheeler. The Tiger purported to be a small sportscar and, while the larger engine allied to the narrow body and low weight certainly gave it good performance, the tandem-type seating, interior layout and controls did nothing to produce a sportscar feel for the driver or passenger.

Although Messerschmitt's unusual steering bar would have been quite familiar to anyone with experience of driving the earlier three-wheelers, it came as a bit of a shock to anyone new to the task. The gearchange was a problem too; there was no synchromesh, and testers often remarked on the uncertainty of getting the right gear at just the right moment with first being "difficult," and reverse sometimes rather too easily found! But for all this the Tg500 was reckoned fun to drive, if not quite the sportscar it was intended to be. Drivers of a cheerful and positive nature would enjoy their Messerschmitts, be they three- or four-wheeled, by taking the advice of the writer in *Motorsport* magazine - who suggested that, to get over the initial shock of the handlebars, you would have to accept that your first few drives would be a series of

erratic swerves; the magazine also advised avoiding potholes.

Despite its larger engine, the Tiger was not particularly noisy to travel in, although vibration could get tiring after a while. The rear seat had room for an adult plus a child, or in the case of some of the advertising photographs, a rather uncomfortable-looking dalmation. The rear cushion was in two parts, and could be hinged upwards so that the whole rear of the cockpit could be used for luggage. There was also a shallow shelf/boot under the tail panel, best reached with the canopy open. A simple heater was available as an optional extra only - it provided insufficient heat to keep the occupants really warm in cold weather, but it did help with the demisting.

By the early 1960s, the small car market had undergone a revolution. This was the age of the Mini - small cars that were real cars in anyone's book were the order of the day. Production of the Messerschmitt dwindled; the very last examples of the Kabinroller three-wheeler and the Tiger four-wheeler left the factory at Regensburg in 1964. Over 50,000 had been built in all. Almost 20,000 of these were the original KR175s and more than 30,000 KR200s, the model which had replaced the KR175 in 1955. Opinions vary as to how many Tigers were made because there are discrepancies between the number that appear to have been built and the

Pages 16, 17, 18 and 19 - This Tg500 exhibits a dramatic two-tone colour scheme which suits it well. Messerschmitt's unusual steering bar came as a shock to anyone more familar with a steering wheel.

number of sets of documents that were issued, but it's likely to have been around 300 only. Whether in three-wheeled or four-wheeled form, the Messerschmitt, with its dome-shaped canopy, gave us one of the most enduring, and endearing shapes of the bubblecar boom - the other being the more spherical Heinkel/Isetta style. Even if some did find a similarity in style between being a Messerschmitt driver and a piece of cheese under a dome, there were plenty who found the experience agreeable - a bit like being in a small aircraft - and, most of all, fun. The car's goggle-eyed headlights and rounded nose gave it character and person-ality, and ensured it a place in many people's hearts.

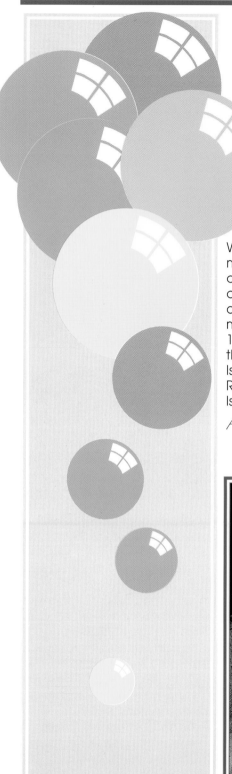

VELAM

2

When Milan-based refrigerator manufacturer Rennzo Rivolta decided that it was time for his company, Isotherm, to branch out, he hit upon the idea of making a small car and, in 1953, gave the world one of the bubbliest of bubbles - the Isetta. Strangely it was not Rivolta himself who made the Isetta so famous, but BMW, the company to whom in 1955 he sold the licence to manufacture the Isetta in Germany.

In the same year, Rivolta also sold the licence to produce his little car in France to the Velam company (a short name - thankfully - for *Societe de Construction de Vehicules legers a moteur*). The Velam-Isetta was extensively rede-

As with the Isetta, the steering column moves out of the way when you open the door - there's a good amount of space inside.

Its fans say the Velam is an altogether nicer shape than the BMW Isetta; it's certainly photogenic.

"It was originally designed by a man who made refrigerators you know."
"If we open the door, does the light come on?"

signed bodywise, especially at the rear. The engine was Iso's 236cc two-stroke, as fitted to Rivolta's own Isettas. A convertible version was offered from 1957.

The little Velam had a lot to offer. It was cheap to buy - being priced at 15 per cent less than the ubiquitous Citroen 2CV. It was cheap to run, fun to drive and had character to boot. But it did not meet with anywhere near the success of the BMW Isetta. In 1958, Velam introduced a luxury version, the Ecrin, but the market was just not there; only 500 of the better-appointed Ecrin versions out of a total of just over 7000 Velams were ever made.

Perhaps the back-up of a company such as BMW helped the Isetta's success - three times as many BMW Isettas were sold in the model's first year than Velam sold in total.

The Velam's bodyshape was much more curvaceous than its teutonic counterpart - a chic off the old block perhaps?

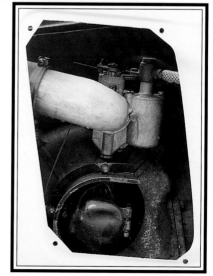

The Velam's engine was Rivolta's own Iso unit as used in the original Rivolta Isetta.

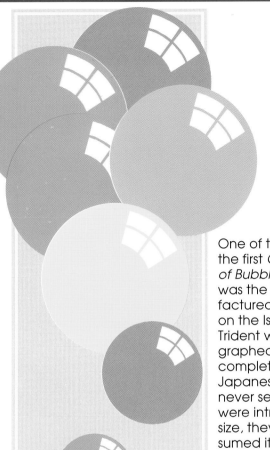

PEEL P50

One of the cars featured in the first *Colour Family Album of Bubblecars and Microcars* was the Peel Trident, manufactured by Peel Engineering on the Isle of Man. While the Trident was being photographed in Windsor, it was completely surrounded by Japanese tourists who, having never seen its like before, were intrigued by it. Seeing its size, they automatically assumed it to be something very new, and were amazed to discover it was built in 1965. Had they seen Peel's P50, which pre-dated the Trident by three years, they would have been speechless, for they would have been looking at the world's smallest car.

Peel Engineering's business was fibreglass moulding. In particular - and being on an island might have had some influence here - they made boats; they also made body parts for motorcycles. The island in question being the Isle of Man, venue for the world-famous TT races. Peel's first foray into the world of car manufacture was in 1955, with the introduction of the Manxman. This was a small three-wheeler, intended for

two adults and either their two (smallish) children or their luggage. The Manxman was capable of almost 90mpg and was supplied in reasonably-priced kit form. However for various reasons the project never really got off the ground and the Manxman disappeared from public view.

The Peel P50 was announced in 1962. The prototype had a single front wheel and twin rear wheels but, by the time the car went into production, this arrangement had been reversed. The P50 was of very simple construction comprising a single seat, surrounded by the fibreglass body which featured a single "cyclops" headlamp centre front. The model was just 135cm long and 99cm wide - about the same size as the average kitchen table. The P50 was powered by a DKW 49cc fan-cooled engine, sited under the seat, which drove the rear wheel via a three-speed gearbox. There was no reverse gear, but as the car weighed only 60Kg the driver simply got out and manhandled the Peel into the desired position with the "reversing handle" fitted at the back.

The P50 was never going to win any medals for comfort or stability - not even a bronze.

Of course, it's a shame not to be able to report that such a brilliant idea - economic and basically practical - was a runaway success. But truth to tell, the P50 did have problems. Driver and engine were in very close proximity, so noise and discomfort had to be endured. The single rear wheel and lightness of construction made the car rather unstable, although some were fitted with extensions on the back corners to help stop them falling over on bends.

The P50 sold at just under £200, but even this reasonable price was not enough to encourage many buyers. Opinions vary as to how many were made, but it was probably in the region of 50. Incidentally, as the cars were hand-built and finished, every example was slightly different. No P50s were built after 1966, by which time Peel were making the Trident, which was slightly larger, had even better fuel consumption figures and was slightly cheaper to buy. Despite these virtues, even less Tridents were sold than P50s.

Peel Engineering, the Isle of Man-based builder of the P50, had a definite leaning towards small cars.

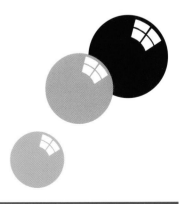

The P50's DKW 49cc engine - too close to the driver for comfort - or quietness.

Cyclops. The P50 is a very, very small car indeed.

Watch your step. The protrusions under the rear were to stop the car rolling over when cornering ...

The P50 was a very basic single-seater with weather protection - the specification list was very short.

The Peel P50 makes any pavement feel like a six-lane highway. Parking is not a problem!

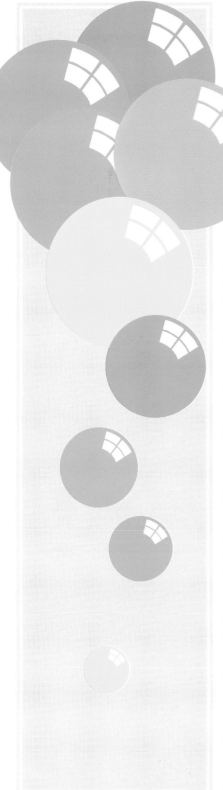

SPATZ & BELCAR

4

Egon Brutsch was one of those eccentrics who, fortunately for the rest of us, turn up from time to time in the motoring world. He was from a wealthy motor racing family and was trained as an engineer. Brutsch was fascinated by small motor cars. He made single-seater one-offs for children and later for adults too. He made several attempts at building scaled-down racing cars too, but without much luck. In 1954, he was to be found developing his new dream; a small, plastic-bodied road car. This was a three-wheeler, capable of carrying three people and powered by a Fitchel & Sachs two-stroke engine. He got as far as producing prototypes for testing and presenting the car - the Brutsch *Spatz* 200 - at the Paris Salon. (Note: Spatz is German for sparrow, so this particular microcar was always going to have pride of place in at least one of our books).

The Spatz was a good-looking little car but, when testing got underway, Brutsch hit a major snag: the car had no chassis and the body was woefully inadequate to take the stresses and strains caused by the loads imposed upon it.

Despite these shortcomings the firm of Alzmetal recognised a glimmer of something marketable in the Spatz and bought the rights to build it. Or rather they didn't buy them because they expected trouble in getting the car on the road and withheld Brutsch's payment cheque. The parties went to court, where the Spatz, as it was then, was ruled totally unroadworthy due to design faults. Of course, the court action guaranteed Brutsch his place in motoring's hall of fame.

Alzmetal undertook a total redesign of the Spatz under the direction of Dr Hans Ledwinka, the Tatra engineer. The totally new Spatz was unveiled in 1955. It had four wheels instead of three and a proper steel chassis, although the engine remained the same. The car went into production the following year in open-topped form. There were no doors, but as the Spatz was very diminutive and the sides low, getting in and out was no more difficult than getting onto a bike. There were plans to market a hard-

Pages 34 & 35 - Quite a pretty car from the rear but the Spatz is strangely styled in that it has front and rear ends of very different character.

Parked alone, the Spatz looks like an ordinary-sized car but, with a passenger, the car's small proportions become clear.

The Fitchel & Sachs
two-stroke engine is
the one item that
remained unchanged
when the car was
redesigned by
Alzmetal.

Plans to build a
gullwing hardtop
version failed
because the
Amphicar's designer
owned the patent for
such doors.

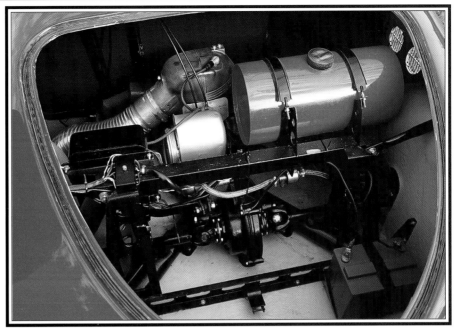

top version with gullwings too, but this would have infringed the patent on such a system owned by Hans Trippel, designer of the famous Amphicar.

In order to make production profitable now that Alzmetal had surmounted the huge problems of getting the car developed and marketable, the Spatz arm of the company looked for a partner and found the Victoria motorcycle company, with which they formed the firm of BAG (*Bayerische Auto-Gesellschaft*).

Specification improvements were made. A larger engine of 250cc improved the top speed to 60mph. This bigger-engined car was badged not as a Spatz, but as the Victoria 250. Then, with the involvement of a further partner from the world of aircraft manufacture, the last models bore the name *Burgfalke* 250. Production ceased in 1957, with approximately 1600 cars having been manufactured.

The Spatz was also manufactured under licence in France and Switzerland, in both cases in the Alzmetal redesigned, three-wheeled form. In France the car was known as the Avolette and in Switzerland as the Belcar. The Belcar project did not last all that long, and only 200 cars were ever made.

To keep them going it's natural that cars such as the Belcar relied quite heavily on their owner's perseverance and ability to carry out maintenance. The Belcar shown in our photographs was once owned by a Swiss nun. Not an

Slightly different priorities prevail in the interior specification department between the Netherlands-registered Spatz made in Germany (above) and the Belcar which was made under licence in Switzerland

ideal means of transport for her one might think, but she was not to be beaten by Egon Brutsch's engineering. When the chassis needed attention, she taught herself to weld and fixed it, doing a not unreasonable job for a beginner. She also adapted the suspension strut from a motorcycle when a unit on the Belcar failed. By all accounts she was a remarkable person, and further proof that owning, maintaining and running microcars has more to do with enthusiasm

Once owned by a nun with attitude, you could say this particular Belcar was kept going by force of habit.

Spatz is German for Sparrow. The expression of the bird in the Spatz badge may represent terror stemming from the unroadworthiness of Brutsch's prototype.

than with just collecting.

Meanwhile, what of Brutsch himself? Was he disheartened? No he was not. He started again, with the *Zwerg*, or Dwarf, available either as a one or two-seater - sales reached double figures. Next came the Mopetta - a very small car indeed based on a moped engine - and the Rollera based on a scooter engine. The Mopetta met with some success - notably in the UK, but the Rollera never caught on. Neither car had the sort of handling that inspired confidence. Next came the *Bussard* (Buzzard) and *Pfeil* (Arrow). Not too many sales here either. Brutsch tried twice more, with the V2 and V2-N - yes, you guessed it. Then it was time for a new venture for Brutsch - something different, non-automotive. Here the story has a happy ending, for Brutsch changed direction completely and began manufacturing prefabricated houses - a venture which brought him the success he had hoped for.

The Belcar project was not a great success - maybe the makers were barking up the wrong tree?

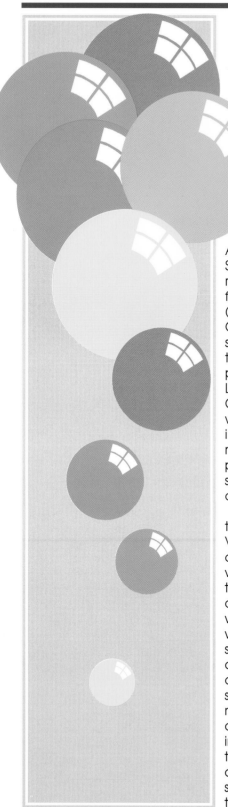

FRISKY

5

At the 1957 Geneva Motor Show, a completely new microcar was unveiled. Manufactured by Henry Meadows (Vehicles) Ltd. to a design by Captain Raymond Flower and styled by Michelotti, this was the four-wheeled, gullwinged prototype of the Frisky family. Later that year, at the Earls Court Show, the Frisky Sport was introduced to the public in spectacular fashion - the racing driver Nancy Mitchell posed for photographs alongside the little Frisky, lending credence to its 'Sport' tag.

The Frisky Sport was a soft-top, equipped with a 328cc Villiers engine. Although it was a four-wheeler, the rear track was substantially shorter than the front, so there was no differential and it was fitted with a live rear axle. The car was both lively - with a top speed of 56mph - and frugal - around 64mpg was par for the course, both of which were strong selling points. Ease of maintenance was billed as another, with only five greasing points on the whole car - two king pins, two rear hubs and the cam gear on the steering. Frisky owners, though, tend to be sceptical about

this one. The suspension was a little on the crude side; friction dampers at the front and hydraulic units at the rear. Extreme care was needed when braking, as the car's nose would lift and it was not unknown for the front wheels to lock up completely.

For a description of the ergonomics of the interior it is impossible to improve upon a first-hand report from someone who we will simply refer to as "an owner." "Suicide type doors were fitted and needed a knack in order to effect entry and exit, many a trouser turn-up was snagged on the protruding choke control which was mounted on the offside wheelarch and the steering column security clip was so positioned that anyone unused to emerging would inevitably take a couple of layers of skin off their left leg." The Frisky's equipment was basic. Instrumentation-wise, all that came as standard was a speedometer, although a rev counter and fuel gauge could be bought as extras. One touch that was quite a luxury at the time, though, was provision for the fitting of a Pye radio.

Top up, the Frisky's styling, especially at the front, is charming, although the top needs to come down to see it at its best.

47

Pages 44-47 - *Maybe the makers wanted you to think it was a bit of a beast but, in reality, the Frisky's "Sport" tag was something of a misnomer.*

Getting out of the Frisky, you can easily lose a layer of skin from your leg or, if you are very careless, a whole leg.

There was another Frisky version available at the same time as the Sport, similar to it but with a hard top, and not unnaturally called the Frisky Coupe. A three-wheeled version was introduced in 1959 - the Frisky Family Three, which was fitted with a 197cc engine, and was the most popular Frisky by virtue of qualifying for cheaper road tax. In 1961, manufacture of the Frisky was

moved to Sandwich in Kent, and although supposedly manufactured until 1964, almost none were sold during the last four of these years. Two new models were introduced at this time, the Prince and the Sprint, but they were unable to revive the flagging Frisky fortunes. Although its production life was short, and only about 500 were ever made, the Frisky did attract a

fair amount of attention and interest. There were plans to produce it under licence in Norway, Holland, Spain, and even Egypt, but all these plans came to nought. The only success in this line came via Gordon Bedson, one of the original design team who worked on the Frisky with Flower. He came across a source of surplus-to-requirement Messerschmitt Tiger

The Frisky's 328cc Villiers engine was advertised as being accessible and easy to maintain with basic tools.

engines in Australia, modified the Frisky Sprint chassis to take them and had them shipped out. The result of his brainwave was known as the Lightburn Zeta.

Basic instrumentation - just a speedo, starter, light and indicator controls and warning lights, but a radio was available too.

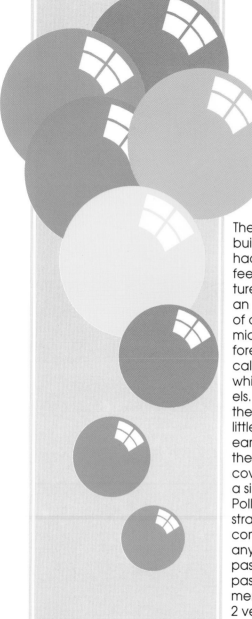

FULDAMOBIL, NOBEL & BAMBINO

The very first Fuldamobils were built in Germany in 1950, and had much of the prototype feel to them. Their manufacturer, Norbert Stevenson, was an expert in the construction of caravans, and built his microcar with these skills to the fore; its bodywork was basically a wooden frame onto which were nailed steel panels. Things improved slightly by the time production of the little three-wheeler began in earnest the following year - the panels were then of covered plywood. The engine, a single cylinder Baker & Polling 248cc unit, was bolted straight onto the floor - not a comfortable arrangement by any standards, for driver or passengers. Another year passed, and more improvements were introduced. The N-2 version had hammered aluminium panels and was fitted with a Fichtel & Sachs 395cc engine. In this form the car returned fuel consumption figures of 60mpg and was capable of good speeds but, even so, less than 400 were sold.

In 1953, Stevenson produced a prototype for another version, this time with more rounded lines and an aluminium body. He sold the licence to produce these cars to the bus manufacturer NWF, which sold the resulting car as the NWF200. Meanwhile, Fulda also started selling their own version, the S-2, at a slightly higher price. From 1955, Fulda introduced the S-4, a less-expensive version with four-wheels: the two rear wheels being set closely together. The S-4 was followed by the slightly improved S-6, which ceased production in 1957. In the same year, Fulda revised their styling completely and introduced a new fibreglass body. This had many advantages, not least reduced weight and, consequently, improved performance. However, even though Fulda had probably developed their best chance of real success with the S-7, sales started to decline. The age of the microcar was over, although the Fulda battled on and was available in Germany right up until 1969.

The Nobel was introduced to the UK in 1958, courtesy of York-Nobel Industries and in particular Cyril Lord, the owner of the company, who financed the project. The

The Fuldamobil's front end styling is less successful than that of its rear end.

Nobel was available either ready-built or in kit form, the latter having the major advantage of a 50 per cent saving on the purchase price. There was a choice of three-wheeled or four-wheeled versions, although the latter had the two rear wheels mounted very close together in order to qualify as a tricycle under British regulations. Whichever version one chose, the engine fitted was a Fichtel & Sachs 200L, similar to that used in the Messerschmitt KR200. This engine was a 191cc single-cylinder two stroke with electrically engaged reverse: it was fitted at the rear of the car and drove the rear wheel or wheels. The Nobel had a chassis of strong steel tubing, to which was attached a sturdy plywood floor. The fibreglass body, which usually came in a two-tone ivory and blue combination, was bonded to the floor. The interior was really very smart. Unusually for a car of its price, the Nobel had a fully upholstered headlining as well as comfortable, well-uphol-stered seats.

One of the major problems with the original Nobel was an alarming tendency for the roof to flex, causing the rear window, and often the roof itself, to crack. To solve this problem, the roofline was redesigned slightly and this second Nobel version, produced from 1959 onwards, was called the Model A. The designers took advantage of the redesign to replace the old-style indicators at the top of the door pillars with safer new indicator lights front and

The Fuldamobil featured very different styling at the front and the rear - a situation common with three-wheelers in general.

rear. Unfortunately, there were still problems inherent in the car. Even the new shape suffered from flexing - the stresses still causing cracking problems around the roof area. Also the cable brakes were inadequate for their task. Despite Cyril Lord's ambitions to build 400 cars a week, it soon became clear that demand was far short of this - in fact, only about 1000 were ever made. The last Nobels rolled off the production line in 1962, although some were still being sold by dealers some three years later.

In addition to the Nobels built in the UK, licences for the construction of cars to the basic Fulda design were sold to foreign manufacturers. The cars appeared in Chile and Argentina (as the Bambi), India (*Hand Vahaar*), Norway, Sweden (Fram King Fulda or FKF), Holland (Hostaco Bambino) and in Greece (first as the Attica and then as the Alta). The licence to build the Fuldamobil in Greece was taken on in 1964 by a plastics manufacturer, which chris-

tened it the Attica. In this guise the car was fitted with a Heinkel single-cylinder engine and was produced in saloon and cabriolet versions. After four years, and with only about 100 units made, the project was sold on to the Alta company. They fitted a Sachs engine and modified the design along more practical - and therefore more marketable - lines. The Alta, while not a huge seller, was quite popular and was made up until 1977.

The Fuldamobil looks a little like an egg, especially in this colour, although it was the Nobel that was more prone to cracking.

The Fulda's interior - plain but functional.

Opposite - The Nobel, produced in the UK under licence by York-Nobel Industries Ltd.

From this angle, the Fuldamobil could be a futuristic amphibian prototype about to take to the water.

The Nobel's day out - "This place is strangely attractive and familiar. Perhaps one of my parents was a dodgem car?"

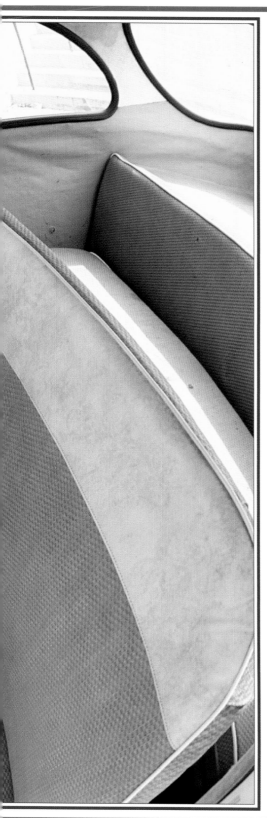

While the Nobel's interior was far from luxurious, York-Nobel realised that to stand any chance of success in the UK market, the car had to be finished well.

The company had aimed to produce 400 Nobels a week, but it soon became clear that there was no demand. The Nobel had reached the end of the road.

Not the most elegant of styling exercises; proportion-wise those fins would probably out-do a Cadillac.

The Bambino - the Fuldamobil as produced under licence in the Netherlands.

The interior is not very different to the Nobel's, but this one benefits from flattering museum lighting at Auto Tron in the Netherlands.

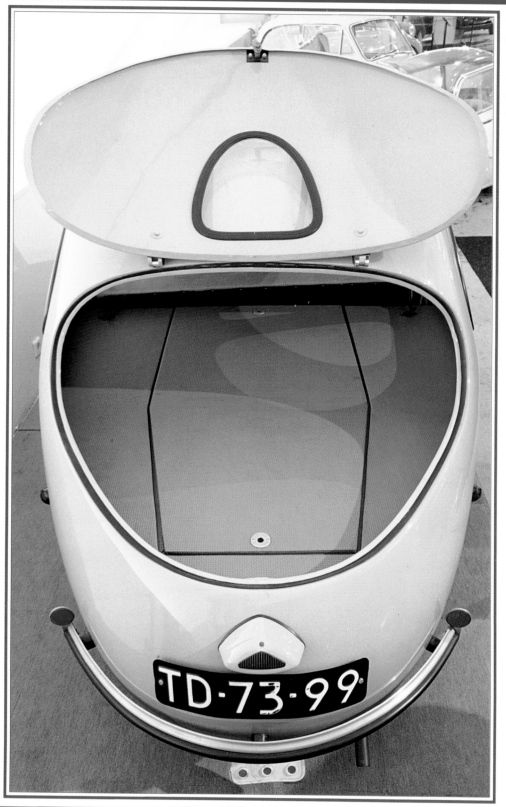

Considering the overall size of the car there's a reasonable amount of stowage space.

BMW 600

The story of the BMW 600 begins with the success of that most bubbly of bubbles, the Isetta. In 1955, Rennzo Rivolta sold the licence to make his little car to BMW. At that time the German company's sales were flagging and its finances in a precarious state; the directors figured that the economic little ISO was just right for the postwar market. They were proved right and, two years later, introduced a four-seater version of the car, the BMW 600. The new little car was presented to the world at the Frankfurt Motor Show in August 1957 and went into production in November of the same year. BMW were aiming the 600 at the gap in the market between two-seaters and full-sized cars.

The car's four-stroke, two cylinder 585cc engine was developed from BMW's 28hp motorcycle unit, but detuned to give 19.5hp at 4000rpm. This successfully provided the additional torque and flexibility needed in a car which, while small in dimensions - just 9ft 6in (2.895m) long by 4ft 6in (1.37m) wide - weighed in at almost half a ton when fully laden. The four-speed 600 had

a top speed of 62mph and returned 50-60mpg, making it a viable choice for longer journeys as well as an ideal car for about town. There was an important technical innovation in the rear suspension department, an advanced and completely new system called the *Schraglenkerachse* - semi-trailing arms that were to become a standard and well-respected BMW engineering feature in the future.

The passenger compartment was inevitably not going to be that roomy, but it was sensibly uncluttered. Leg and head room was good, and the seats comfortable. There was space for luggage behind the rear seat, which could also be folded estate-car fashion to provide a conveniently large load area, or removed entirely for even more space.

Although the pre-production 600s had been quite austere inside, by the time production started BMW felt confident enough of the car's potential to improve its specification considerably. So the 600 came with combined armrests and side pockets, a floor-sited handbrake and a conventional dashboard, beneath which the spare wheel was mounted. The engine was reached through a hinged panel below the rear window. The air which cooled the engine could be directed into the passenger compartment to provide heating when required although, when the temperature dropped to freezing, the quantity of air was sufficient only to defrost and demist - with very little left over for cold feet. Summer ventilation was provided by the three sliding windows.

Access to the front seats was via the side-hinged front door. As with the Isetta, the steering wheel swung away with the door and was fitted with a second universal joint which kept it well out of the driver's way as he climbed in and out. The door was fitted with a counterbalance spring to hold it open too. Even so, *Autocar* magazine's 1958 reviewer worried about other cars parking too close to the front door, a situation which might effectively lock you out of your car. They also fretted over how a woman might get in and out gracefully. But, unusually for a journal renowned for its thorough, scientific and no-nonsense approach, the writer con-

A rather more elegant forerunner of today's dealership window-sticker.

cluded that "... it has real character - indeed, its owner might come to regard it as something slightly more personal than just utility transport." In plain English, the

The Isetta, the 600 and the 700 helped BMW re-establish after a bad patch: the company became a force to be reckoned with.

The BMW 600 - aimed at the market between two-seaters and bigger saloon cars.

BMW 600 was likely to get a pet name and be treated like one of the family!

The rear passengers got in through a door on the right-hand side; this never varied as no right-hand drive models were made. The UK market was given serious consideration but was judged not large enough to merit the investment. This was a correct assessment; only a few dozen were ever sold into the UK. In Germany, the car's 3890DM (£330) price tag placed it ideally between Fiat's 500 and 600. However, in the UK, the purchase price of £676, of which over 30 per cent was purchase tax, meant it could not have hoped to compete against the more reasonably priced home-grown cars. The 600 was quite popular in the USA though, where it was fitted with larger, sealed-beam headlamps and modified bumpers to meet the USA's legal requirements. 600s were also made under licence in Argentina during 1960, under the name of De Carlo.

The 600 continued in production until 1959, by which time the small car market was filling out and competition was increasing. However, the model sold extremely well, with almost 35,000 being made in total. BMW moved on to produce the 700, a model based on the 600. The Isetta, the 600 and the 700 had enabled

Plenty of room in BMW's biggest bubble.

BMW to get back on its feet and develop the new models which would establish the company as a major manu-facturer of saloon cars.

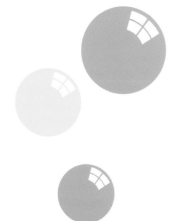

The 600's four-stroke power unit was derived from
BMW's proven 28hp motorcycle engine.

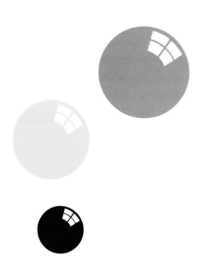

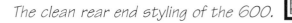
The clean rear end styling of the 600.

Entrance to the rear of the 600 is via the single door on the righthand side.

Access to the front seat is via a front door: similar in principal to the Isetta.

Like the Isetta, the 600 came in charming colour schemes very evocative of their era.

The ingenious universal-jointed steering column: the steering wheel moves out of the way when the front door is opened.

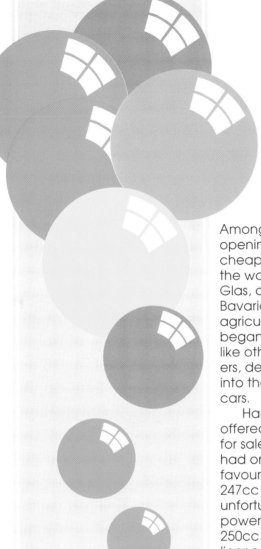

GOGGOMOBIL

Among those who spotted an opening in the market for cheap, reliable transport once the war was over was Hans Glas, a businessman from Bavaria, whose line had been agricultural machinery. He began to make scooters and, like other scooter manufacturers, decided to branch out into the manufacture of small cars.

Hans Glas GmbH first offered their little Goggomobil for sale to the public in 1955. It had one important point in its favour from the start; its tiny 247cc engine, although unfortunately rather underpowered, brought it within the 250cc limit for cheaper road licences in Germany. The car was a four-wheeler, built of steel on a platform chassis. Its transversely mounted two-stroke engine, which was designed by Glas himself, was sited at the rear and drove the rear wheels through an integral gearbox. It produced 14bhp and, as the car weighed only 770lbs, both performance and consumption figures were good. The car was reported to be a respectable performer, reaching 50mph (80kph) and return-ing 50 miles to a gallon (4.5 litres) of fuel.

Initial reaction to the little Goggomobil four-seater was very enthusiastic - 5000 were sold almost immediately, with nearly 25,000 of the model being built before it ceased production the following year. In 1957 Glas introduced an improved design, the coupe. This was a two-seater with a much less boxy and much more modern shape than the original. It was available in a choice of two engine sizes, 293cc and 392cc, and there was the option of a Getrag preselect gearbox too. This newer version was known as the Mayfair in the UK, while the original was called the Regent. A few convertibles, vans and pick-ups were built, but never really caught the imagination of the public.

Hans Glas set his sights higher again the following year, building 600cc and 700cc cars. Goggomobil production passed the 100,000 mark, but the car's days were numbered. Glas began to fit water-cooled, four-cylinder engines - costly to tool up for and produce and not condu-cive to making the car as

inexpensive as possible. Glas found himself in severe financial straights. His company was eventually taken over by BMW, which, within a year, halted production of all but the small Goggomobils. Licences were granted for Goggomobil production in other countries in an attempt to boost funds. The most notable success was in Spain, where the small Goggo was extremely popular. A strange saloon/van hybrid was manufactured there too. Meanwhile in Australia, Bill Buckle fitted his own design of fibreglass open-topped sports body to the Goggo chassis - a futuristic but wonderfully overstyled creation known as the Goggomobil Dart.

BMW kept the smaller Goggomobil on the books for a while longer. By the time production ceased in 1969, 280,000 Goggomobils had been made. However, that was not quite the end of the Goggomobil story; there are licences still operative in Germany to this day, and there is an enthusiastic band who have converted their little Fiats to run on little Goggo engines. Although perhaps not as instantly recognisable as a Heinkel, Isetta or Messerschmitt, the Goggo was a much loved and popular little car which still commands a dedicated following.

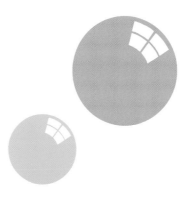

Although production finished in 1969, it wasn't quite curtains for the Goggomobil; some of the production licences are still in effect today.

Opposite - Unlike many microcars, the Goggo got into a decent run of production - almost 25,000 were made.

The interior is plain but stylish, with plenty of leg and headroom.

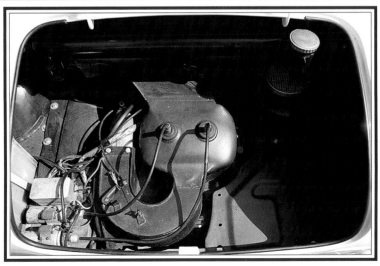

The Goggo's tiny 247cc engine kept it in the "cheaper to run" league, but as the car was so light, performance was still good - unless fully laden.

A conventionally-shaped car in small proportion - similar in this respect to both the Fiat 500 and the French-built Vespa 400.

A nomadic Goggo; I've been everywhere and I've got the badges to prove it!

SCOOTACAR
Mk1 & 2

The postwar boom in the market for reliable, affordable motoring brought some spectacular successes - the Vespa Scooter and the Citroen 2CV for example - but also some spectacular failures. The Rodley was one of the latter. Refreshingly unaffected by concepts such as styling, the Rodley had a nasty habit of spontaneous combustion, due to the complete enclosure of its rather large engine in the its rear end. After production that just made it to double figures, the Rodley disappeared in a puff of smoke in 1956, leaving Henry Brown, its designer, high and dry.

Brown joined the Hunslet Engine Company, a Leeds-based locomotive manufacturer, as new products manager and, within the year, he had produced the prototype of a tiny, four-wheeled car which had none of the obvious disadvantages of his first attempt. The prototype was

Scootacar controls would have been familiar to anyone who had ridden a scooter.

powered by an Anzani engine which suffered severe over-heating problems but, by the time the Scootacar went into production in 1957, it was fitted with a Villiers 197cc two-stroke unit. The renamed car had been restyled too. It was now a three-wheeler, two at the front and one at the back, with a single nearside door and capable of carrying two adults, one behind the other, with the alternative of two smallish children fitting in the rear. The Scootacar was well-built with a sturdy chassis incorporating a steel floor upon which the fibreglass body was fitted. It was inexpensive - £350 in 1958 - and qualified for low-band road tax; it was also economic - 80mpg at average speeds. Capable of 45mph, the Scootacar was not uncomfortable and was easily driven; with the exception of the scooter-style handlebars, all the controls were of car-type. The original version of the Scootacar has become

Pages 86 & 87 - Locomotive salesmen could afford to sit back and wait for orders to come down the line; unfortunately, this approach was not appropriate for Scootacars and sales suffered as a consequence.

known, in retrospect, as the Mk1.

The Mk2 Scootacar was first produced in 1960. It looked different to the Mk1 by being more rounded at the front and with an elongated rear end. The seating arrangement had been changed to a more comfortable single seat, offset slightly to the right, for the driver and twin seats at the rear for passengers. *Motor Cycling* magazine, testing the Mk2 Scootacar in March 1961,

Scootacar MkI seating arrangement; the driver's back support was negligible and the rear passenger could either sit astride the seat or perch to one side.

Scootacar MkI - the logo; prone to break when being cleaned.

The works - the Villiers two-stroke engine was accessed through the seat box.

was quick to appreciate the small stature of their test vehicle. "... the asset of easy parking took much of the heartburn out of everyday driving in London's frustrating congestion. Narrowness made threading one's way into gaps just too easy; shortness turned mere openings into parking spaces." Did they really mean heartburn or heartache? We will never know. The tester set the prospective owner's mind at rest regarding the unstable looks of the Scootacar. Although its proportionate tallness made it look as if it would topple over on corners, the truth was that it handled very well with no roll and no hint of wheel-lifting, even when driven at its limits. It also promised to be as easy to maintain as a two-wheeler and cheap to keep. The magazine summarized as follows: "The 1961 Scootacar sets a new standard in accommodation for the small three-wheeler. With this go excellent braking, good handling and a sufficiently vigorous performance to make this little vehicle a very practical proposition for the family man who seeks comfortable transport at the minimum cost."

Henry Brown parted company with Hunslet in 1960. 1500 Scootacars had been sold in all. In view of the rave reviews and popularity of the concept - there was nothing basically crude or unstylish about the Scootacar - one is left won-

The Scootacar Mk1. Big enough for full-sized people too.

The Scootacar Mk2 had revised styling.

The engine of the Mk2 Scootacar was reached by removing the rear seat base.

Indicators are placed up near the roofline on both versions. The wiper mounting point changed from windscreen top on Mk1 to windscreen bottom on Mk2.

dering whether a better sales and marketing operation might have yielded a real success story. The salesmen charged with selling the car were more used to selling railway locomotives - not a hard-sell market at that time - and there was hardly any advertising to back up the product. Although there was a good brochure that made the most of the car's best features, there was no real pro-

motion; Hunslet didn't even take stands at the motorcyle show. The year after Brown left, the company launched another Scootacar version - the Mk3 De Luxe Twin. This was fitted with a 324cc engine and was blessed with greatly improved performance. But it was expensive to make, and could not be sold at a good enough profit to make production worthwhile for very long. Only 20 Mk3s were sold. Henry Brown moved away from microcars, but did not lose interest in them, approaching several companies with ideas. Brown wrote to Clive Sinclair at the time of the C5 project, offering his services. We can only wonder if the course of that particular project would have changed if he had become involved.

There is an interesting story about the Scootacar's toughness, as told by Henry Brown to Michael Worthington-Williams of *Practical Classics* magazine. "Scootacars were tested at the MIRA track and the firm used a relay of drivers

Scootercar Mk2's one-piece casting badge, making cleaning and polishing a lot less hassle.

to traverse the Belgian pave section of the track as part of the varied test track sequence. One of the drivers was the assistant works manager, John Wilkinson, a keen motorcycle trials rider. His instructions were to drive the vehicle as fast as it would go, but to keep it under control. John took over and immediately reduced the lap time substantially. During a run over the pave, however, he lost control and left the track, striking a low grassy bank. The Scootacar dug its nose in, rolled forward onto its roof and completed a somersault! John then regained the track without stopping and completed his circuit. The whole episode was observed by the officer on duty in the watch tower, who couldn't believe his eyes. The roll contributed nothing to the test programme however. When the vehicle was later checked over it was found to be one inch lower than standard, but otherwise undamaged."

Mk2's seating changed for the better - more comfortable for the driver and more legroom for the passenger.

The rear end of the Mk2 Scootacar is much more elongated than that of the Mk1.

Opposite - Although it looks as though it will topple over at the slightest provocation, the Scootercar is actually surprisingly stable.

Just my size - a pity I'm not old enough to drive yet.

Dear Reader,
We hope you enjoyed this Veloce Publishing production.
If you have ideas for other books on automotive subjects, please write to tell us.
Meantime, Happy Motoring!

There are other Colour Family Albums covering Citroen 2CV, Citroen DS, Vespa scooters, Lambretta scooters, VW Beetle and Bubblecars & Microcars. More titles are in preparation.